MW00598575

Play Piano with...
Katie Melua
Norah Jones, Delta Goodrem
Christina Aguilera
Vanessa Carlton
Alicia Keys & DJ Sammy

Wise Publications
part of The Music Sales Group

London / New York / Paris / Sydney / Copenhagen / Berlin / Madrid / Tokyo

Published by
Wise Publications
8/9 Frith Street, London W1D 3JB, England.

Exclusive Distributors:
Music Sales Limited
Distribution Centre, Newmarket Road,
Bury St. Edmunds, Suffolk IP33 3YB, England.
Music Sales Pty Limited
120 Rothschild Avenue, Rosebery, NSW 2018, Australia.

Order No. AM980694
ISBN 1-84449-634-1
This book © Copyright 2004 by Wise Publications.

Edited by Lucy Holliday
Compiled by Nick Crispin
Music arranged by Paul Honey
Cover photographs courtesy of LFI and Redferns
Printed in Great Britain by Printwise (Haverhill) Limited, Haverhill, Suffolk

CD Recorded, mixed and mastered by Jonas Persson
Backing vocals by Elly Barnes & Alison Symons
Piano by Paul Honey
Guitars by Arthur Dick
Bass by Paul Townsend
Drums by Brett Morgan
Cello by Julia Graham
Flugel Horn by Andy Gathercole
Clarinet by John Whelan
Violin by Cathryn McCraken

Your Guarantee of Quality
As publishers, we strive to produce every book to the highest commercial standards.
The music has been freshly engraved and the book has been carefully designed to
minimise awkward page turns and to make playing from it a real pleasure.
Particular care has been given to specifying acid-free, neutral-sized paper made from
pulps which have not been elemental chlorine bleached.
This pulp is from farmed sustainable forests and was produced with special regard for the environment.
Throughout, the printing and binding have been planned to ensure a sturdy,
attractive publication which should give years of enjoyment.
If your copy fails to meet our high standards, please inform us and we will gladly replace it.

www.musicsales.com

Beautiful

Words & Music by Linda Perry

I am beau-ti-ful,___ in ev-'ry sin-gle way.__ Yes,
You are beau-ti-ful,___ in ev-'ry sin-gle way.__ Yes,
We are beau-ti-ful,___ in ev-'ry sin-gle way.__ Yes,

words can't bring me___ down._____ Oh,___ no._____
words can't bring you___ down._____ Oh,___ no._____
words can't bring us___ down._____ Oh,___ no._____

1.

To Coda ⊕

So don't you bring me down_ to-day.

2.

No mat-ter what_ we do,_____ no mat-ter what_ we say,

we're the song in-side_ the tune,_____ full of beau-ti-ful mis-takes._

And ev-'ry-where_ we go,_____ the sun will al-ways shine,

D.S. al Coda

but to-mor-row we might a-wake,_____ on_____ the oth-er side._

Born To Try

Words & Music by Delta Goodrem & Audius Mtawarira

Call Off The Search

Words & Music by Mike Batt

2. And I won't spend my nights gaz - ing_____ at the stars up____ in the

sky, won-der-ing____ if____ love will____ pass me____ by.____ Now_____

_____ that I've found you I'll call off the search.____

Out____ on my own____ I would____ nev - er have known____ this

call off the search.

Now that I've found you I'll

call off the search.

Now that I've found you I'll

call off the search.

Don't Know Why

Words & Music by Jesse Harris

To Coda ✦

Gm⁷ · C⁷ · F⁷sus⁴ · B♭ · B♭⁷ · Gm⁷ · C⁷

I don't know why___ I did-n't come,___ I   don't know why__ I did-n't__

F⁷sus⁴ · B♭ · B♭maj⁷ · B♭⁷ · E♭maj⁷ · D⁷

__ come.__   2. When I saw___ the break__ of day__

Gm⁷ · C⁷ · F⁷sus⁴ · B♭ · F¹¹ · B♭maj⁷ · B♭⁷

I wished that I___ could fly__ a way,___   'stead of kneel-ing in

E♭maj⁷ · D⁷ · Gm⁷ · C⁷ · F⁷sus⁴ · B♭

the sand,   catch-ing tear-drops in my__ hand.__ My

19

heart is___ drenched in_____ wine.___

But you'll be___ on___ my____ mind___

for___ ev - er.___ - er.___

Piano solo

Verse 3:
Out across the endless sea
I will die in ecstasy
But I'll be a bag of bones
Driving down the road alone.

My heart is drenched in wine etc.

Verse 4:
Something has to make you run
I don't know why I didn't come
My field is empty as a drum
I don't know why I didn't come
I don't know why I didn't come
I don't know why I didn't come

Heaven

Words & Music by Bryan Adams & Jim Vallance

1. Oh, I'm think-ing a-bout our young-er years._____ There was

How Come You Don't Call Me

Words & Music by Prince

Al-ways thought you'd be_____ by my side, pa-pa,___ now you're gone._____ "And I'm

not tryin' to hear that s**t." What I wan-na know ba-by, if what we had was good,___

how come you don't call me a-ny-more?_____

Vocal ad lib.

Verse 2:
Still light the fire on the rainy night
Still like it better when you're holding me tight
Everybody said
Everybody said that we should never part
Tell me baby, baby, baby why
Why you wanna go and break my heart.

All I wanna know baby *etc*.

The Closest Thing To Crazy

Words & Music by Mike Batt

A Thousand Miles

Words & Music by Vanessa Carlton

♩ = 94

2 bar count in:

1,3. Mak-ing my way down town, walk-ing fast;
(Verse 2 see block lyric)

fac-es pass,_ and I'm home-bound.

And I, I don't wan-na let you know.

I, I drown in your me-mo-ry. I, I

don't wan-na let this go. I, I don't.

And I still need you, and I still miss you.

Verse 2:
It's always times like these
When I think of you
And I wonder if you ever think of me.
'Cause everything's so wrong
And I don't belong
Living in your precious memory.
'Cause I need you
And I miss you
And now I wonder:

If I could fall into the sky *etc.*

10/04 (52734)

ABBA
Chiquitita
Dancing Queen
Mamma Mia
Money, Money, Money
Waterloo
The Winner Takes It All
Order No. AM963314

The Beatles
All You Need Is Love
The Fool On The Hill
Good Day Sunshine
Hello Goodbye
Hey Jude
Lady Madonna
Let It Be
Penny Lane
Order No. NO90698

Coldplay
Amsterdam
Clocks
Everything's Not Lost
Politik
The Scientist
Trouble
Order No. AM979132

Coldplay, Toploader,
plus... David Gray, Robbie Williams, Muse, Elliott Smith & Moby
Achilles Heel
She's The One
Son Of Sam
Sunburn
This Year's Love
Trouble
Why Does My Heart Feel So Bad?
Order No. AM970849

Play Piano *with...*
all these great artists

Elton John

Can You Feel The Love Tonight
Candle In The Wind
Goodbye Yellow Brick Road
I Guess That's Why They Call It The Blues
Rocket Man
Song For Guy
Your Song
Order No. AM955526

Norah Jones

Cold Cold Heart
Come Away With Me
Don't Know Why
I've Got To See You Again
The Nearness Of You
One Flight Down
Shoot The Moon
Turn Me On
Order No. AM84229

Diana Krall

Baby, Baby All The Time
Devil May Care
Fly Me To The Moon
(In Other Words)
The Night We Called It A Day
Only Trust Your Heart
Peel Me A Grape
Straighten Up And Fly Right
Order No. AM979957

The music book...

Authentic solo piano arrangements with vocal line, full lyrics and chord symbols.

The CD...

Full 'soundalike' instrumental backing tracks for each song plus tracks without the piano so you can play along!

All titles available from good music retailers, or in case of difficulty please contact the distributors:
Music Sales Limited,
Newmarket Road, Bury St. Edmunds, Suffolk IP33 3YB
Tel: 01284 725725; Fax: 01284 702592
www.musicsales.com

CD Track Listing

Full performance demonstration tracks...

1. Beautiful
(Perry) Famous Music Publishing Limited.

2. Born To Try
(Goodrem/Mtawarira) Sony/ATV Music Publishing (UK) Limited.

3. Call Off The Search
(Batt) Sony/ATV Music Publishing (UK) Limited.

4. Don't Know Why
(Harris) Sony/ATV Music Publishing (UK) Limited.

5. Heaven
(Adams/Vallance) Rondor Music (London) Limited.

6. How Come You Don't Call Me
(Prince) Universal/MCA Music Limited.

7. The Closest Thing To Crazy
(Batt) Sony/ATV Music Publishing (UK) Limited.

8. A Thousand Miles
(Carlton) Universal Music Publishing Limited.

Backing tracks only (without piano)...

9. Beautiful
10. Born To Try
11. Call Off The Search
12. Don't Know Why
13. Heaven
14. How Come You Don't Call Me
15. The Closest Thing To Crazy
16. A Thousand Miles

To remove your CD from the plastic sleeve,
Lift the small lip on the side to break the perforated flap.
Replace the disc after use for convenient storage.